Social Studies for Primary
Grade 2
Workbook

Myself, my family, my school

Cynthia Smith

All Rights Reserved. No part of this publication may be reproduced, stored in a retrieval system, or transmitted, in any form or by any means, electronic, mechanical, photocopying, recording or otherwise, without the prior permission in writing from the author and publisher.

The author and publisher are still awaiting a response from some copyright owners and will acknowledge permission at the first opportunity.

Table of Contents

Using this book……………….....3
Families………………….…..….4
Looking at buildings………..…..6
Looking at churches………...…..8
Looking at roads and docks……..10
What is a community?...................12
Things we do in our community…14
Showing tourists around…………16
Changes over time……………….18
Looking at the weather…………..20
The farmer……………………….22
The police officer………………...24
The firefighter…………………….26
Doctor and nurse…………………28
The dentist………………………..30

People who keep our community clean……………………………….32
People who make our clothes……….34
People who teach us……………….36
Other people who help us…..……..38
Leaders in our community………..40
We must help others………………42
Being polite and friendly………….44
Welcome tourists………………….46
Planning a special project…………48
Joining special groups…………….50
Protecting living things around us…..52
Let's make a map……………..…..55
Work cited ……………………..…..57

Using this Book

This workbook is to be used in conjunction with The Bahamas' Ministry of Education second grade curriculum. All of the topics and relevant notes came from the curriculum. Teachers should teach the lessons first to students and then allow them to answer the questions about each topic.

The following should be taken into consideration when teaching the lessons in this book.

-Students are engaged in hands-on activities so that they can see the practical part of the lessons.

-Field trips should be taken where possible.

-Guest speakers should be invited to share their knowledge of the topic/s.

-Lots of visuals should be used when teaching the lessons.

To be better able to deliver an engaging lesson, teachers can go to the website: *www.bahamaseducationexpress.com*. On this site, they will find the following:

-PowerPoint lessons for all lessons in this book

-Short videos for most lessons

-Additional worksheets for lessons

Remember teachers, "*children learn by doing*." It is our prayer that you enjoy using this book to help educate the students of our Bahama Land.

Families

Some families are big. Some are small. Some have both mother and father. Other families have just one parent. Some families have children. Others have no children.

A community is made up of many kinds of families.

Date: _____

1. Why do you think some families only have one parent? [2]

_____

_____

Look at pictures and then answer the questions. [4]

2. How many families are there in this community? [1]

_____

3. How many fathers? [1]

_____

4. How many children? [1]

_____

5. How many people live in this community? [1]

_____

Looking at buildings

Look at this community.

What kinds of buildings can you see? When you look, you will see schools, hospitals, the post office, churches, hotels, banks, restaurants, bakeries, liberties, and police stations.

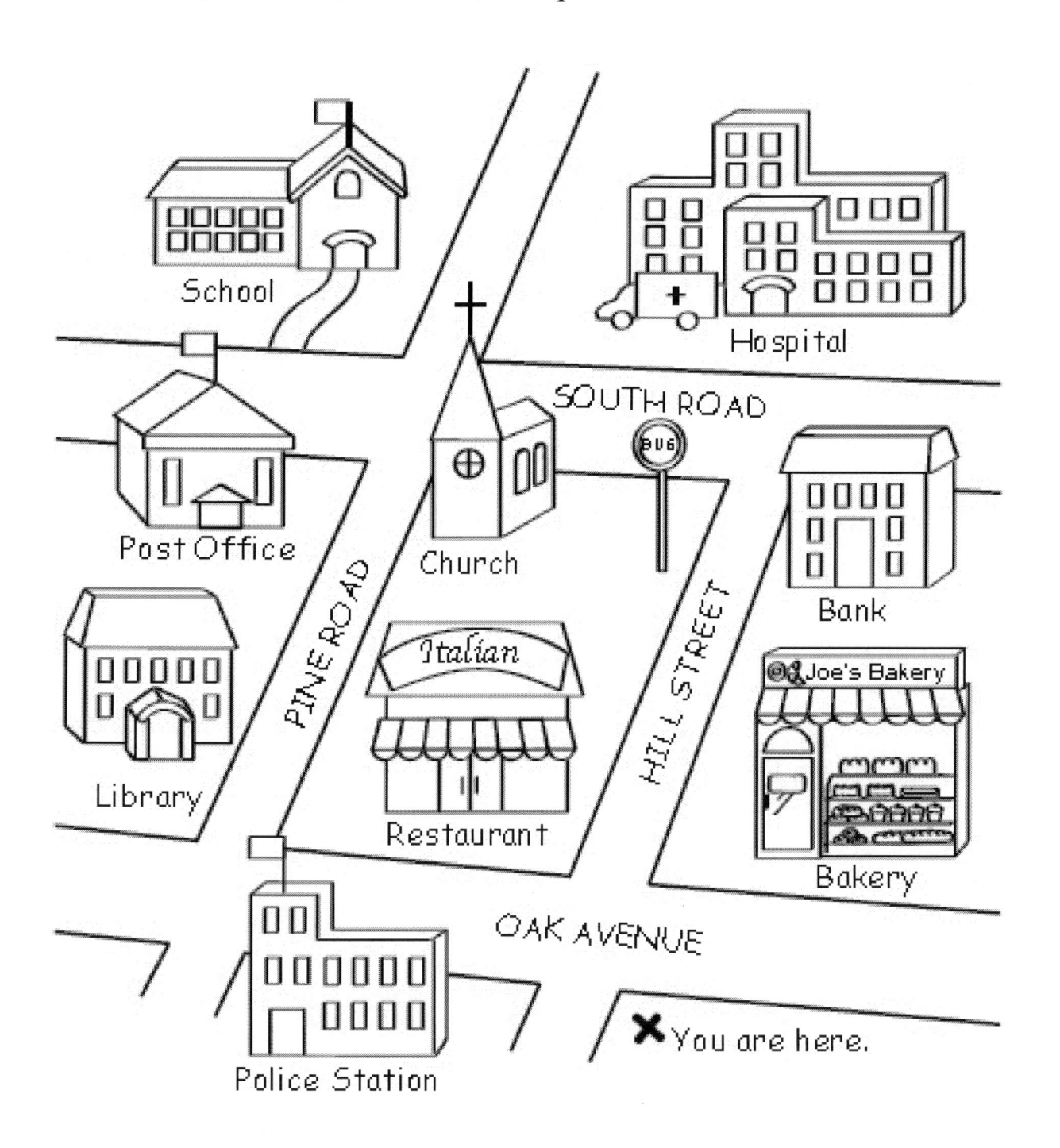

Date: _____

What does your community look like? Draw a picture of your community. Draw as many buildings and write the names of the buildings. [10]

Looking at churches

We worship God in churches. There are many ways to worship. There are many different churches in our communities.

church

Date: _____

1. What church do you attend? [1]

   _____

2. List THREE churches in your community. [3]

   _____

   _____

   _____

3. List FOUR things you do when you go to church. [4]

   _____

   _____

   _____

   _____

Looking at roads and docks

Roads are important to all of us. They help people to get from place to place. They help to move goods.

Roads link your community to the **harbours**. Harbours are also very important. Boats **dock** there to load and unload goods.

Mailboats help to link the **Family Islands** to New Providence. Family Islands depend on the mailboats for goods and services. Nassau, the capital city of The Bahamas, is in New Providence. Look at the mailboats at Potter's Cay dock in Nassau, New Providence. They go to many of the Family Islands.

Potter's Cay Dock

Date: _____

1. Look at these two roads. Write TWO ways how they are different. [2]

_____

_____

_____

2. Write TWO reasons why roads are important. [2]

_____

_____

3. Write the name of the harbour in your community. [1]

_____

_____

4. Name TWO kinds of boats that dock at harbours? [2]

_____   _____

What is a community?

Where a group of people live, play, and work together is called a community.

families   plus   buildings

roads   plus   harbours

equals
a community

Date: _____

1. Where is your community? [1]

   _____

2. How did it get its name? [1]

   _____

   _____

3. Write THREE sentences to tell what your community looks like. [3]

   _____

   _____

   _____

4. What do you like about your community? [1]

   _____

   _____

5. Write TWO ways how your community helps you? [2]

   _____

   _____

   _____

Things we do in our community

There are many things we do in our community. Look at the pictures and see some of the things happening in each one.

Date: _____

Think about FIVE other things that we do in our community and write about it.

_____
_____
_____
_____
_____
_____
_____

Showing tourists around

The Bahamas is a friendly community. Look at how we welcome our visitors. Visitors from other countries are **tourists**. They come here on holidays and vacations. We show them interesting things in our community.

Date: _____

1. List TEN places in your community to show to a tourist. [10]

_____   _____

_____   _____

_____   _____

_____   _____

_____   _____

2. Who are visitors? [1]

_____

_____

3. What are the TWO times that most visitors come to our community? [2]

_____

_____

4. Collect pictures of these places from question one and make a booklet with them. [10]

Changes over time

People make changes all the time. Communities grow. New places are built. New roads are made. The trees and plants grow and die. Some places change quickly. Other places change slowly.

Look how this community has changed.

Date: _____

List EIGHT new things you see in the picture B. [8]

_____
_____
_____
_____
_____
_____
_____
_____

2. What are some of the changes in your community that you have seen or heard about? [5]

_____
_____
_____
_____
_____

Looking at the weather

The weather is what we see or feel in the air around us.

Some of the things we feel and see are:

How hot it is
How cold it is
How dry it is
How often does it rain?
Is the wind blowing?
Is it calm?
Are there any clouds in the sky?

Weather can change quickly. Or it may stay the same for a long time.

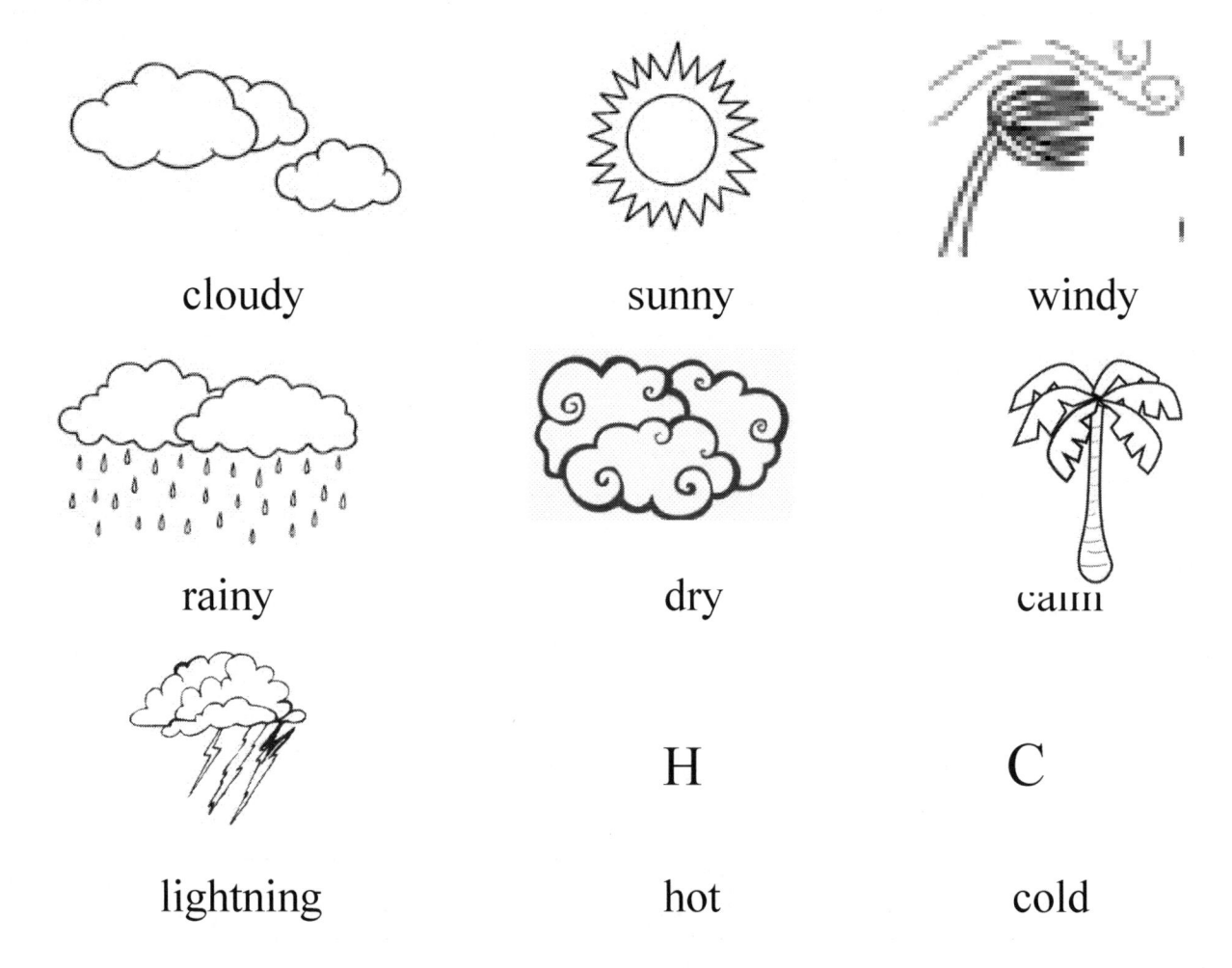

cloudy	sunny	windy
rainy	dry	calm
lightning	hot	cold

Date: _____

1. The weather on Sunday was cloudy, wet, and windy. This is how we show it.

Sunday

2. In the chart below, draw the correct weather symbols for every day of the week. [5]

The weather this week				
Monday	Tuesday	Wednesday	Thursday	Friday

3. What kind of weather do you like? [1]

_____

4. What kind of weather do you dislike? [1]

_____

5. Write TWO sentences about the weather where you live. [2]

_____

_____

The farmer

We need food for good health. Fresh fruits and vegetables are very good for us. They are grown on farms and in yards. Some farmers sell their **produce** at the market, to food stores, and hotels.

Date: _____

1. Write the names of the fruits in the picture. [5]

_____   _____

_____   _____

_____

2. Write the names of the vegetables you can see. [5]

_____   _____

_____   _____

_____   _____

3. Draw a picture of a market stall of fruits and vegetables. [10]

The police officer

The police officer is your friend and my friend. Police officers make sure that we obey the law. They help to keep our community safe. Would you like to be a police officer?

Date: _____

1. There are four phrases in the box that tells how the police officer helps. Write the correct phrase under each picture. [4]

(a) make sure everything is safe	(b) visits schools
(c) catch criminals	(d) make sure we cross the road safely

_____   _____
_____   _____
_____   _____

_____   _____
_____   _____
_____   _____

The police officer makes sure that I _____ the _____ [2]

The firefighter

The firefighter wears a special **uniform**. The uniform shows that he or she **belongs** to a special branch of the police force. Firefighters wear some things to protect them.

Date: _____

1. Look at the picture and write **ONE** sentence to tell what the fire fighter is doing. [1]

_____

2. Why do we need firefighter? [1]

_____

_____

3. What should you do if you see a place on fire? [1]

_____

4. What phone number should you dial if you see a fire? [1]

_____

5. How can you help stop fires from starting? [1]

_____

_____

Doctor and nurse

When we are not well, we visit the hospital or the clinic. Here we are seen to by a nurse and a doctor.

When we are sick, we need **medicine**. We need help when we have an **accident**. Sometimes we may need an **operation**. Then we are **admitted** to a hospital. We are admitted to hospital for many reasons.

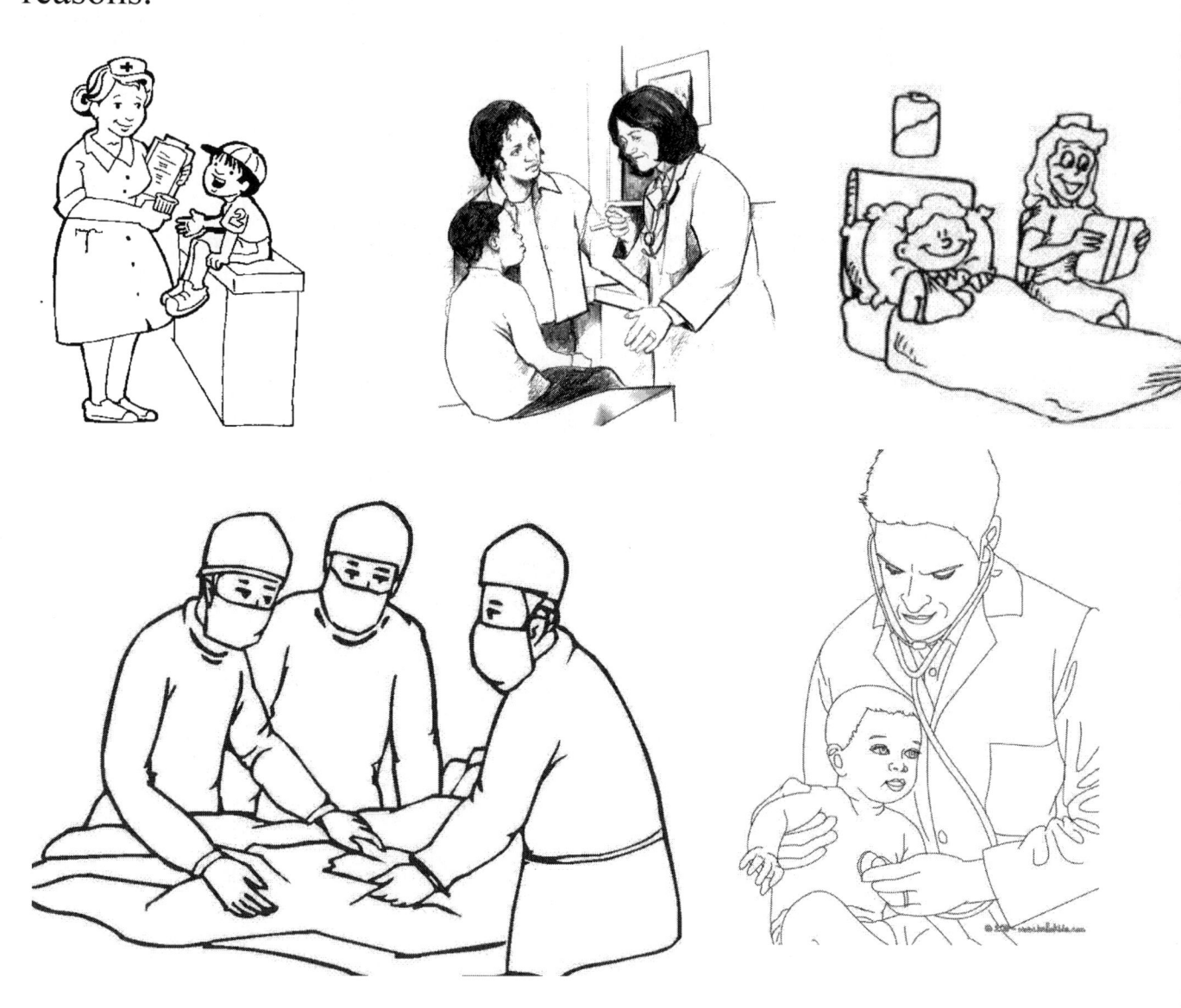

Date: _____

1. How are doctors and nurses helping in the pictures on page 28? Write FIVE ways.

_____
_____
_____
_____
_____

2. Look at the pictures below and write THREE other ways that doctors and nurses help.

_____   _____   _____
_____   _____   _____

3. Write TWO sentences to tell how you can keep well and avoid injury. [2]

_____
_____

The dentist

The dentist checks our teeth. We must visit the dentist twice a year. The dentist sterilizes each instrument after using it. We must brush our teeth at least twice a day. We should also floss our teeth.

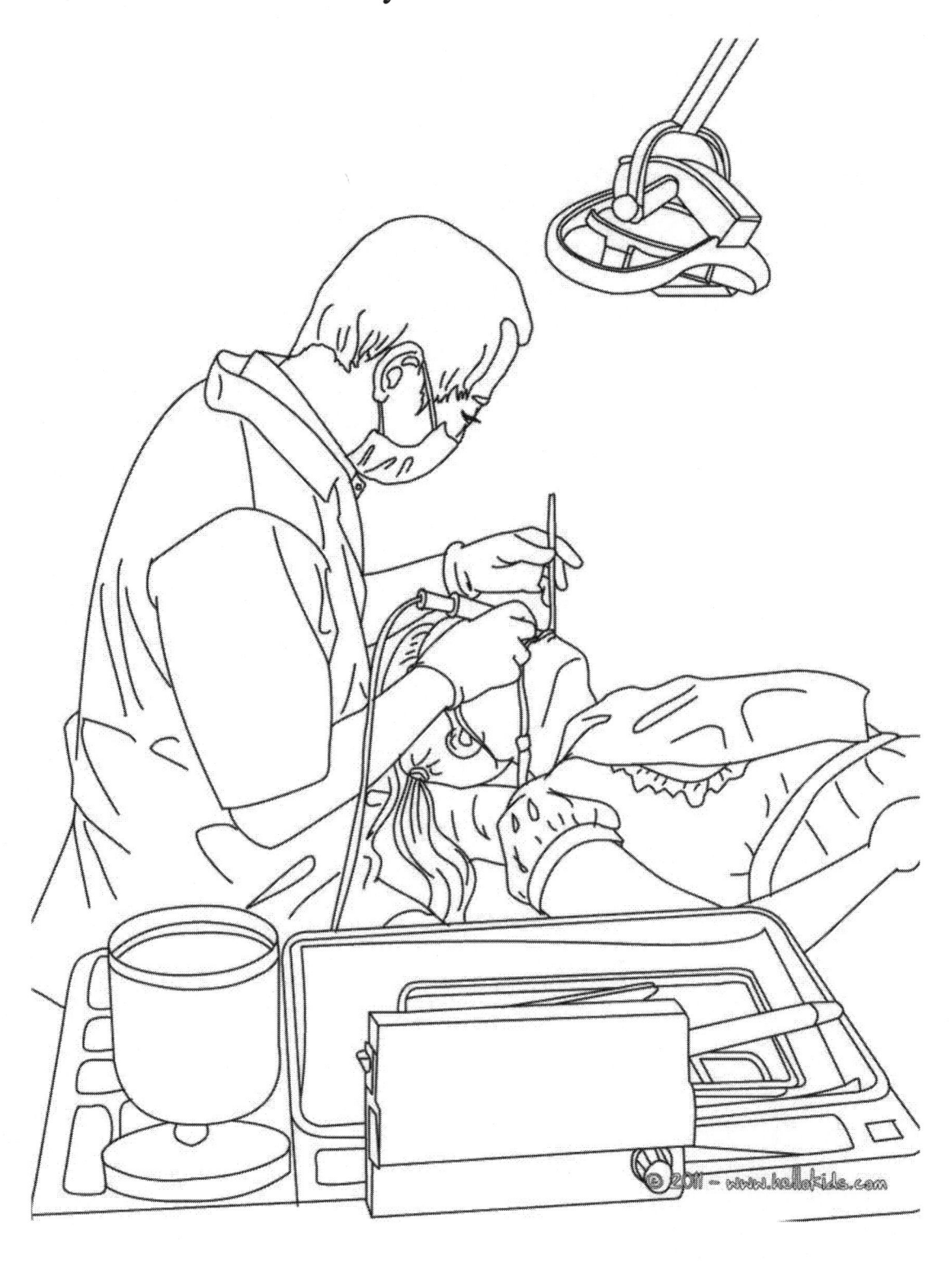

Date: _____

1. Write TWO things we should do to take care of our teeth. [2]

_____

_____

_____

2. Why do we visit the dentist? [1]

_____

3. Why does the dentist sterilize his or her instruments after use? [2]

_____

_____

4. Write a sentence about what is happening is the picture below. [1]

_____

_____

People who keep our community clean

street cleaner

garbage collector

yard man/gardener

Date: _____

1. How do these people help to keep our community clean and healthy? Write TWO ways. [2]

_____

_____

_____

2. Write TWO things that would happen if we did not have these workers? [2]

_____

_____

3. Write THREE ways how we can help to keep our community clean? [3]

_____

_____

_____

People who make our clothes

materials	makers	clothes
	dressmaker	
	tailor	

Synthetic   Cotton   Wool   Silk

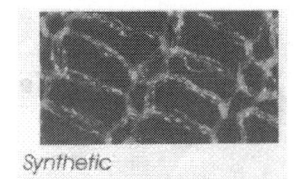

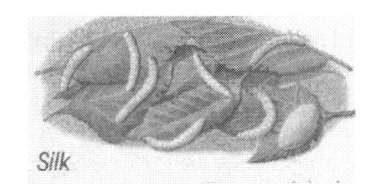

The materials our clothes are made from comes from the cotton plants that give us cotton. The sheep that gives us wool, the silkworm that gives us silk and raw materials that gives us synthetic.

35

Date: _____

1. Look at the picture. Write the correct names from the box under the correct pictures. [3]

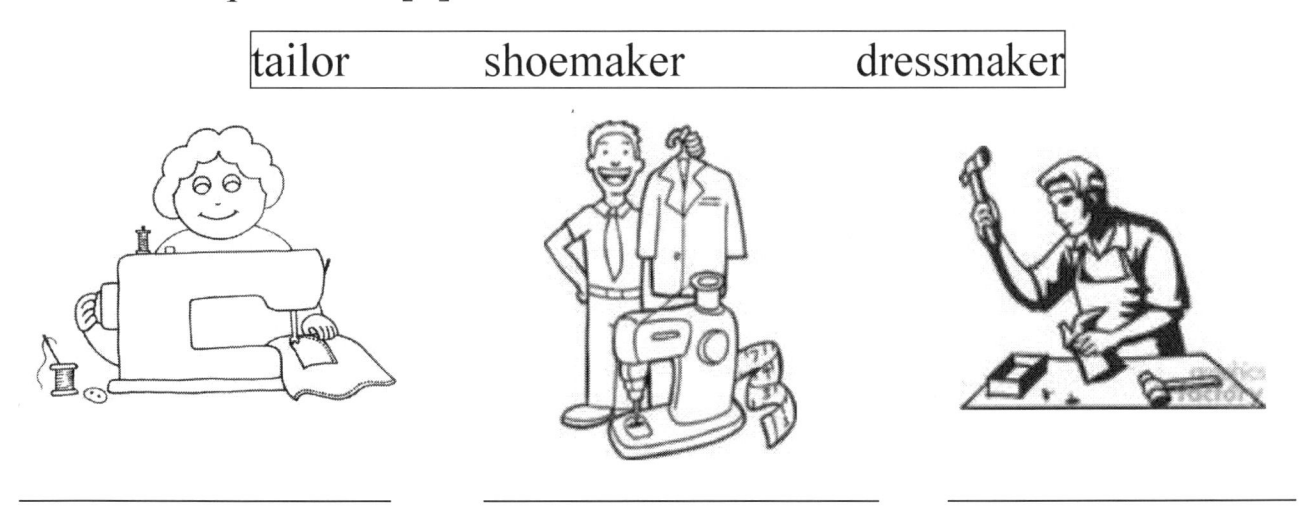

| tailor   shoemaker   dressmaker |

_____   _____   _____

2. Write a word from the box under the correct clothing to tell the material it is made from. [4]

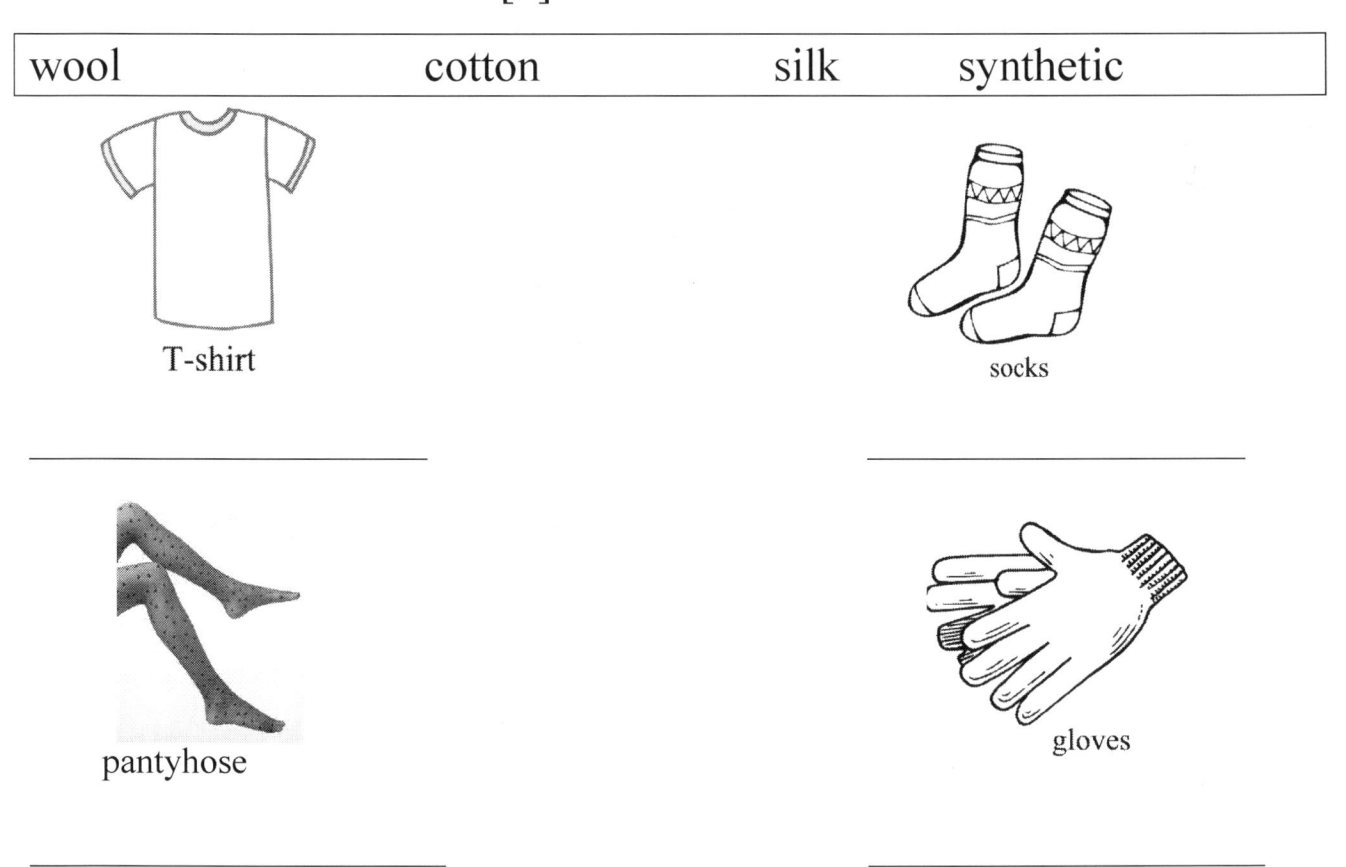

| wool   cotton   silk   synthetic |

T-shirt

socks

_____   _____

pantyhose

gloves

_____   _____

People who teach us

The teacher helps you learn to read and write. He or she teaches you about the world. Your teacher is very important.

Date: _____

1. Write TWO reasons why your teacher is important to you. [2]

_____
_____
_____

2. Name TEN of the teachers in your school and tell what grades they teach. [10]

Name	**Grade**
_____	_____
_____	_____
_____	_____
_____	_____
_____	_____
_____	_____
_____	_____
_____	_____
_____	_____
_____	_____

3. Write the names of THREE other persons who help you learn. [2]

_____   _____

_____

Other people who help us

There are many workers in the community. They have special skills. Here are some of them.

chef

chemist

bus driver

veterinarian

beautician

farmer

Date: _____

1. Match the names of the workers with the jobs that they do. Write the letter on the line.

lifeguard or beach warden ___		A. helps us to find the right book in the library
security officer ___		B. makes furniture and other things from wood
carpenter ___		C. prepares medicines for us when we are sick
librarian ___		D. helps keep swimmers and our beaches safe
pharmacist ___		E. protects buildings in our community from thieves

Find out more about people who help us. Choose a worker in your community. Ask them questions on a worksheet. Tell the class what you find out.

Leaders in our community

The hurricane damaged the community. Trees were uprooted. Boats were broken. Roofs were blown away. Some houses were gone. There were dead animals and fish all around. There was no electricity. The people had to help themselves.

The preachers, the principals, the island Administrator, the police officer, the farmer, and a Red Cross volunteer got together. They set up a committee to plan what to do. They were leaders. Each person had a special job.

The preacher made a list of the damages. The farmer was in charge of moving trees. The principal made the school into a home for the people with no houses. The Red Cross volunteers cooked food for the hungry people. Everyone helped the leaders with these jobs.

Date: _____

1. List the leaders in the community.

   _____   _____

   _____   _____

   _____   _____

2. List FIVE ways the leaders help their community. [5]

   _____

   _____

   _____

   _____

   _____

3. Name TWO leaders in your community. [2]

   _____   _____

4. Can you name one hurricane that has damage your community?
   [1] _____

5. Write TWO things that makes someone a leader. [2]

   _____

   _____

We must help others

In our study so far, we have learnt about people who help us. Remember how the doctor, the police officer, and the street cleaner help us. People in a community **co-operate**. They work together and help each other. Look at the picture below. Everyone is helping to clear up after the **hurricane**.

Date: _____

1. Write THREE things that you can do in your community. [3]

_____

_____

_____

2. With a friend, plan how you can help someone in need. Write some of your plans on the lines below.

_____

_____

_____

_____

_____

Being polite and friendly

Look at Bent.
Look at the teacher, Mrs. Bain.
They are so polite and friendly.
They respect each other.
They help each other.

We must be polite to everyone we meet. We must be polite when we use the telephone. Let's pretend to use the telephone. Someone be John. Someone be Gloria. Read what they say.

John: Hello.

Gloria: Hello. Is this John? This is Gloria. May I please speak to Karen?

John: I am sorry Gloria, Karen is not at home. Would you like to leave a message for her?

Gloria: Yes, please. Please tell her that I called. I will call back later.

John: I will give her your message.

Gloria: Thank you. Goodbye.

John: Goodbye.

Date: _____

Write a sentence to tell how you can be polite in the following situations.

at home:

_____

_____

at church:

_____

_____

at school:

_____

_____

on the telephone:

_____

_____

Welcome tourists

There are many ways we welcome tourists to our country. We entertain them.

We make them laugh.
We are friendly.
We welcome them to our homes.
We have lots of fun together.
We show them around our community.

Date: _____

Imagine there are tourists visiting your school. Plan a way to entertain them. Write your ideas down on the lines below and share them with the class.

_____
_____
_____
_____
_____
_____
_____
_____
_____
_____
_____
_____

Planning a special project

These children are doing a special project.

They collect empty cans.
The cans will be recycled.
The community will be cleaner.

We should all help people who are in need. These children are collecting food for people who are hungry, the Red Cross and the Salvation Army.

We need to plant trees. They give shade and protect the soil. These children are planting 20 trees.
This is their project.

This wall was covered with graffiti or unwanted pictures. The students help to paint it. The community will look cleaner and better.

1. What can you do with used cans? [1]

2. After collecting food goods, name TWO organizations that can benefit from the food goods. [2]

3. Write TWO things trees give. [2]

4. Is graffiti good for our community? [1]

5. Write a reason for your answer. [2]

Joining special groups

In our community children join several groups such as the Pathfinders, the Brownies, the Cub Scouts, and the Boys and Girls Brigades. These groups help people in the community.

Date: _____

1. Look at the picture and name SEVEN things the group members are doing in the picture. [7]

_____
_____
_____
_____
_____
_____
_____

2. Name THREE special groups in your community. [3]

_____
_____
_____

3. Tell one thing each of these groups do for the community. [3]

_____
_____
_____

4. Which group do you belong to? Or which group would you like to join? [1]

_____

Protecting living things around us

Animals, birds, fish, coral and trees are all living things. Living things must be **protected**. Trees are beautiful. Trees protect the soil. Birds are beautiful. They spread seeds from place to place. Fish, coral, and living things must be taken special care of. They provide food.

We must keep the sea clean. Fish will choke on garbage. Garbage will **destroy** our sea life.

Leave the birds alone to fly freely.

Keep litter away from trees and shrubs. Litter may start a fire.

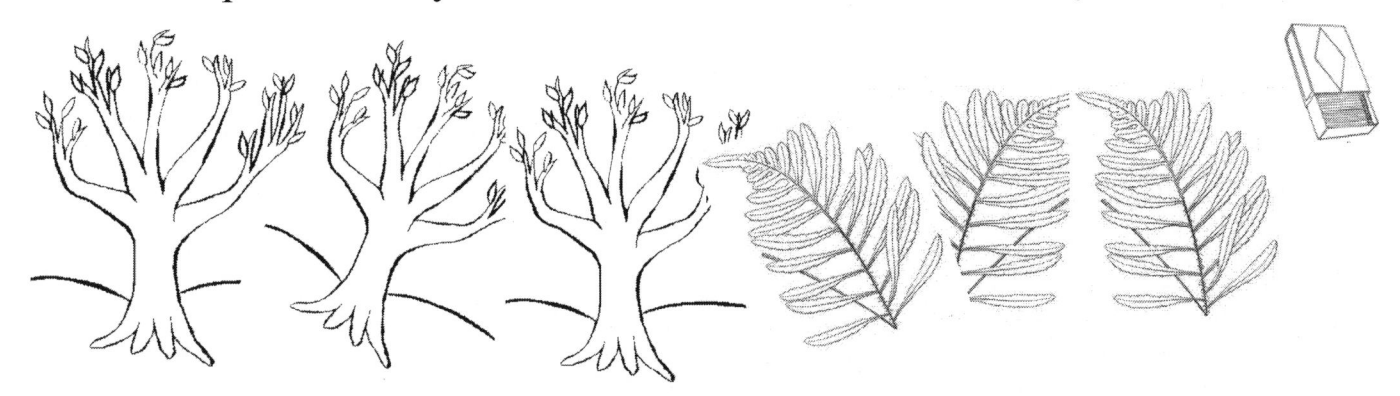

Protect all animals from harm.

We must protect the living things around us. If we do not, they will disappear.

Date: _____

1. Make a list of SIX rules to protect living things on your island. [6]

_____
_____
_____
_____
_____
_____

2. List FIVE ways you can keep your island clean and green. [5]

_____
_____
_____
_____
_____

3. Use the letters for the statements on the right and match them with the living thing on the left. [5]

Living things	Ans.	How they protect
fish		A. We protect the soil
garbage		B. We spread seeds from place to place
litter		C. We provide food
trees		D. We destroy the sea life
birds		E. We start fire

Let's make a map

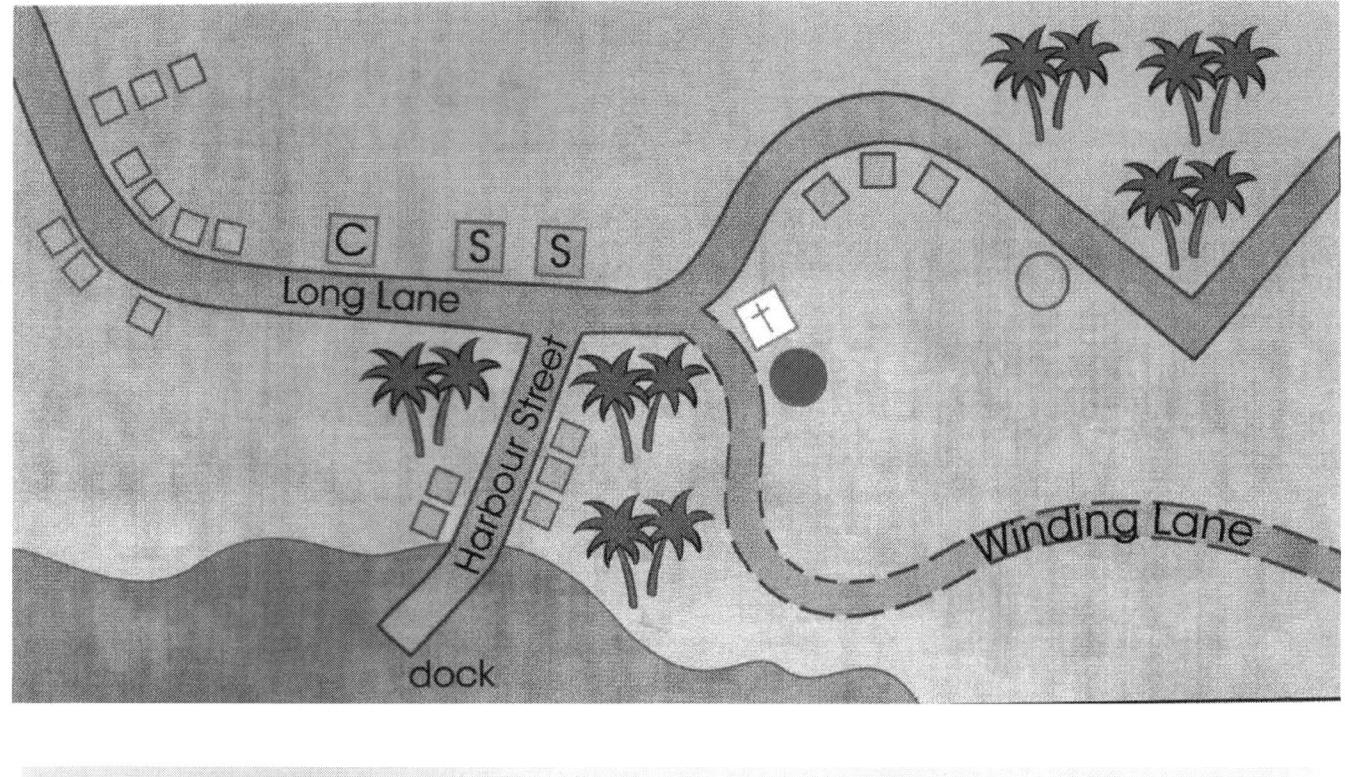

▬ road	▬ track	S shop	☐ house	C clinic
✠ church	● police station	🌴 trees	● school	

The **map** above shows a small community. It has a **key**. The key is one part of a map. The key tells you what the symbols mean.

Date: _____

1. How many keys does this map has? [1]
_____

2. Which road has a church and a school? [1]
_____

3. Which road has only houses on it? [1]
_____

4. How many houses are there in the community? [1]
_____

5. How many schools are in the community? [1]
_____

6. At the end of which road will you find the dock? [1]
_____

Work Cited

Department of Education. (1997). *Commonwealth of The Bahamas, Ministry of Education Social Studies Curriculum Guideline*s (Grade Levels 1and 2)

Made in the USA
Columbia, SC
20 April 2023